Big thi

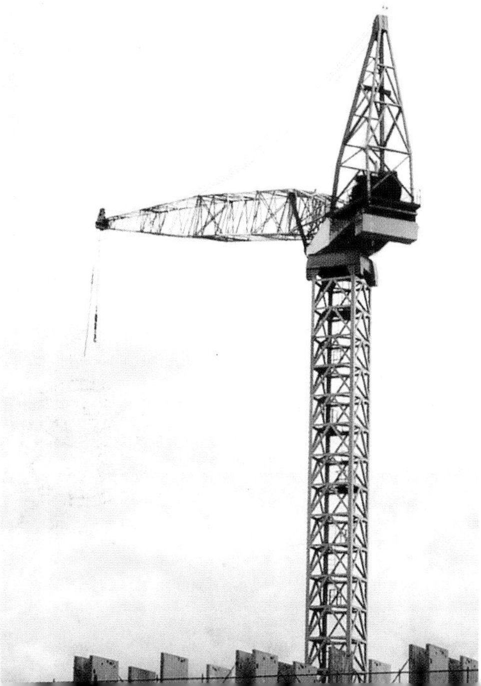

A truck is big.

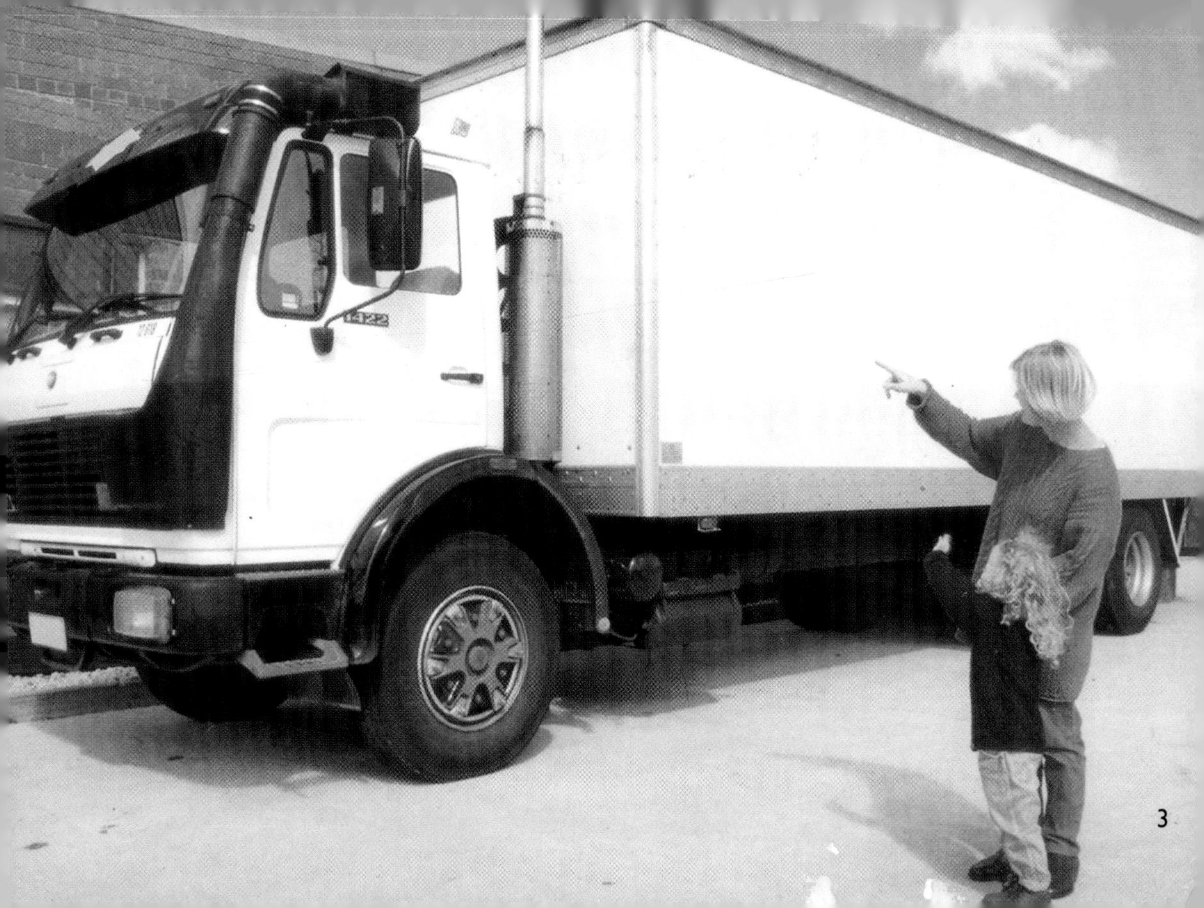
1422

A bulldozer is big.

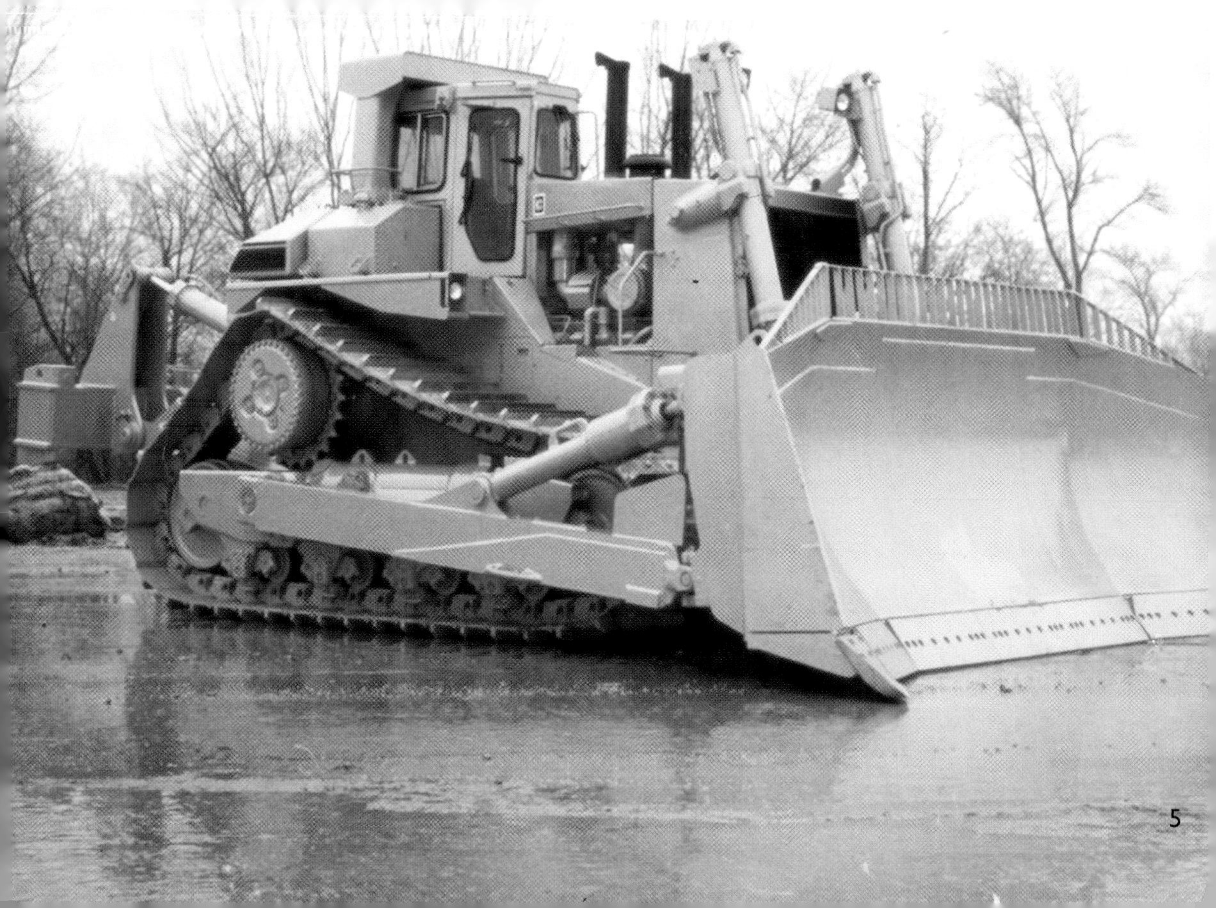

An ambulance is big.

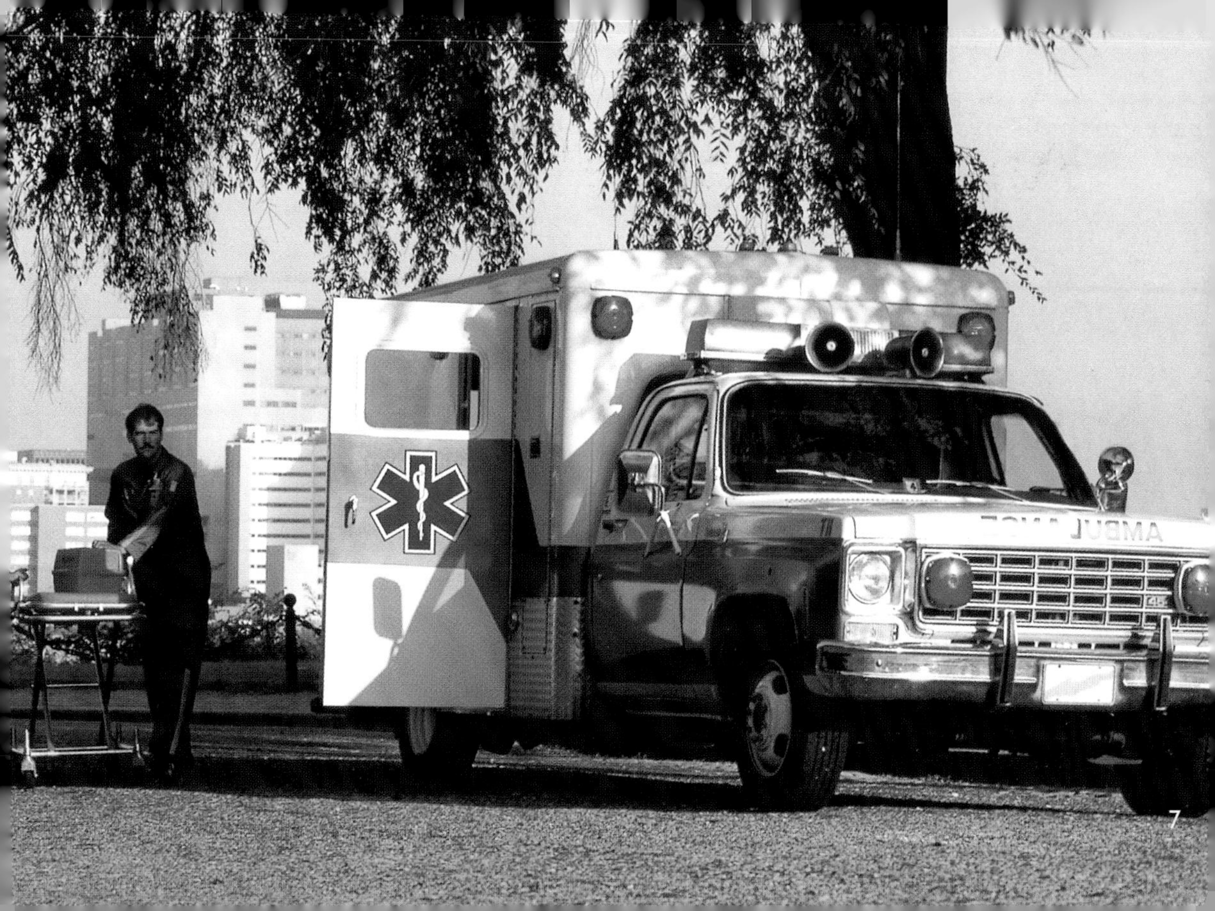
AMBUL

A fire engine is big.

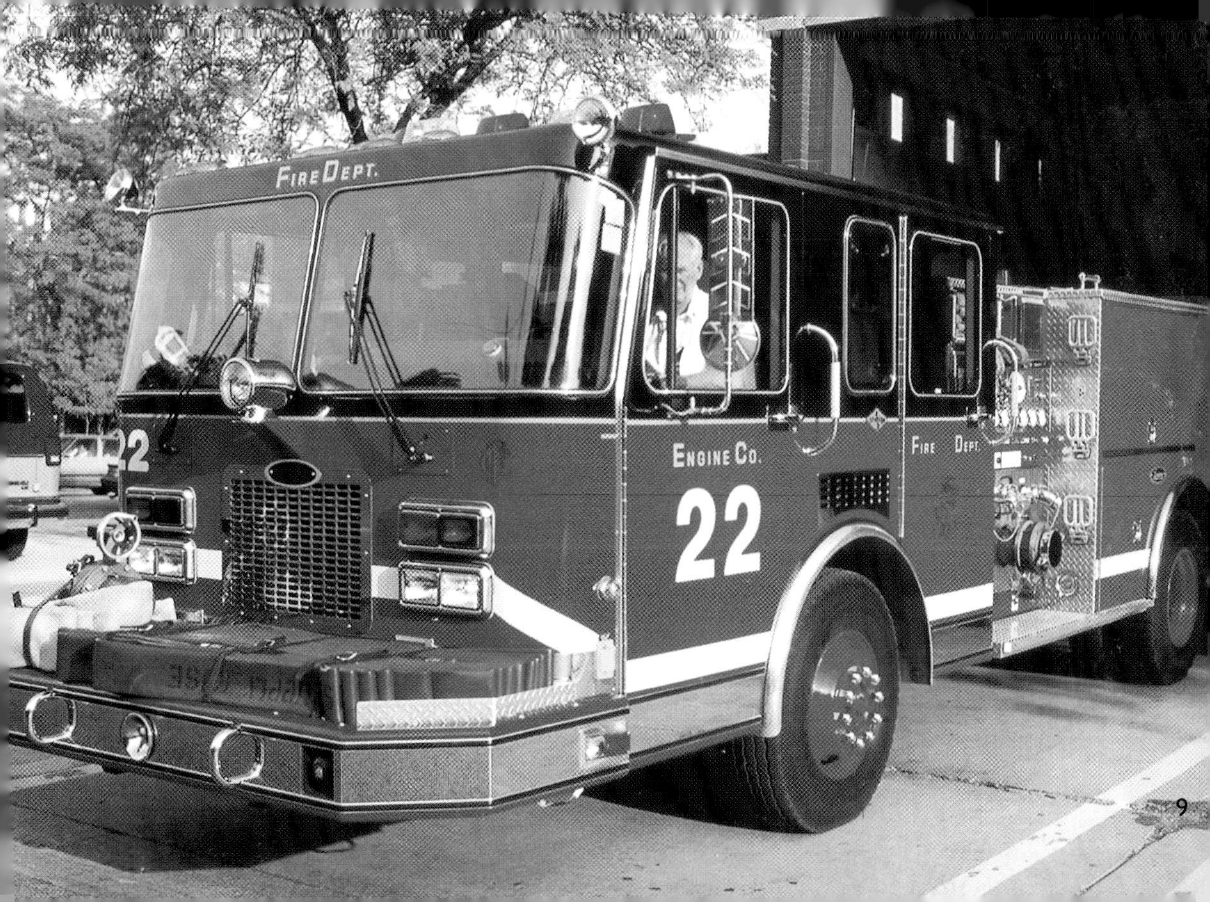
FIRE DEPT.
ENGINE CO.
22
FIRE DEPT.
22

A bus is big.

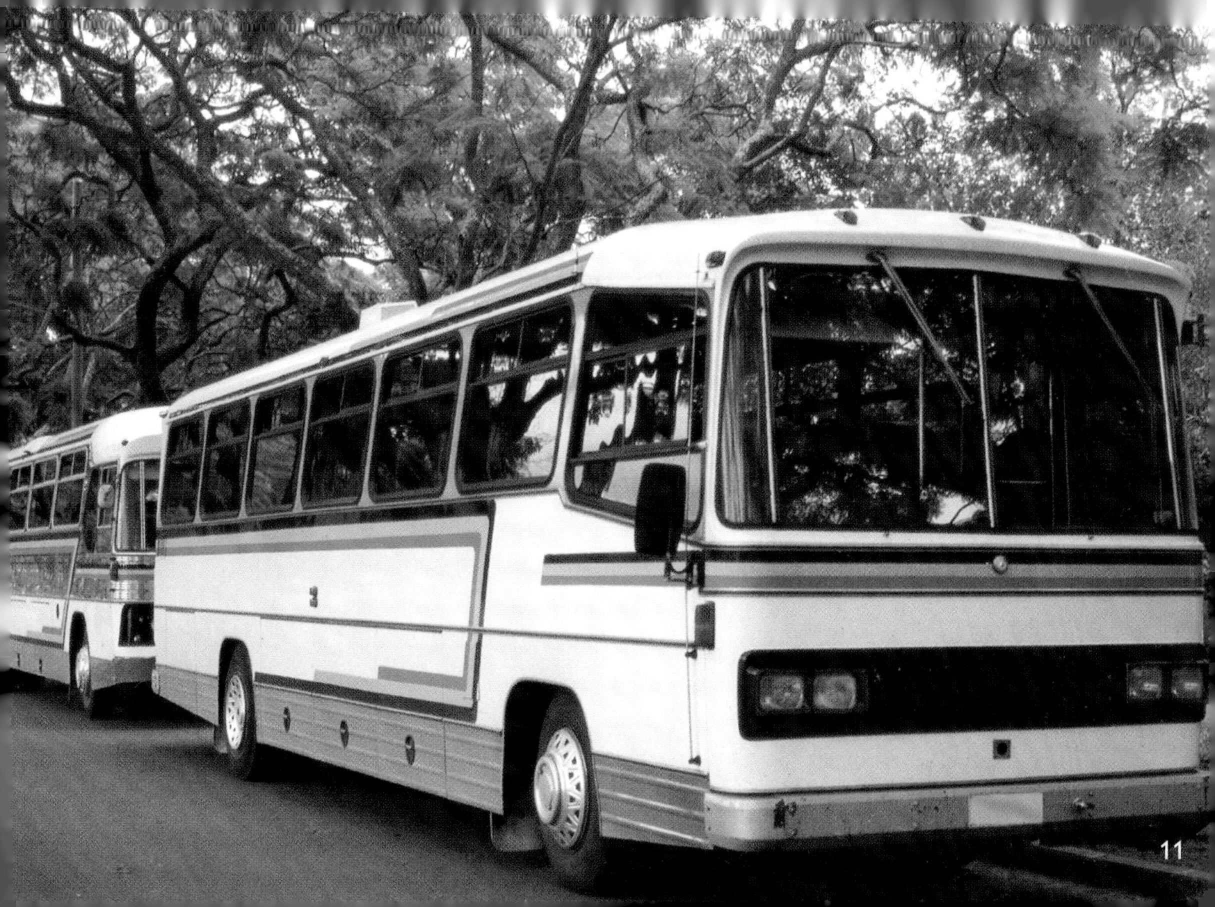

A crane is big.

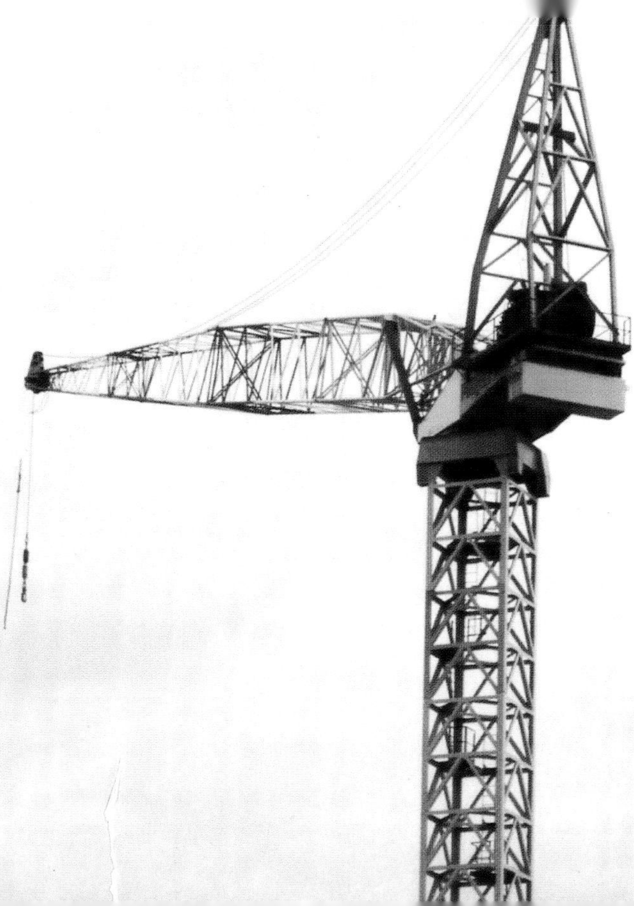

A ship is big.

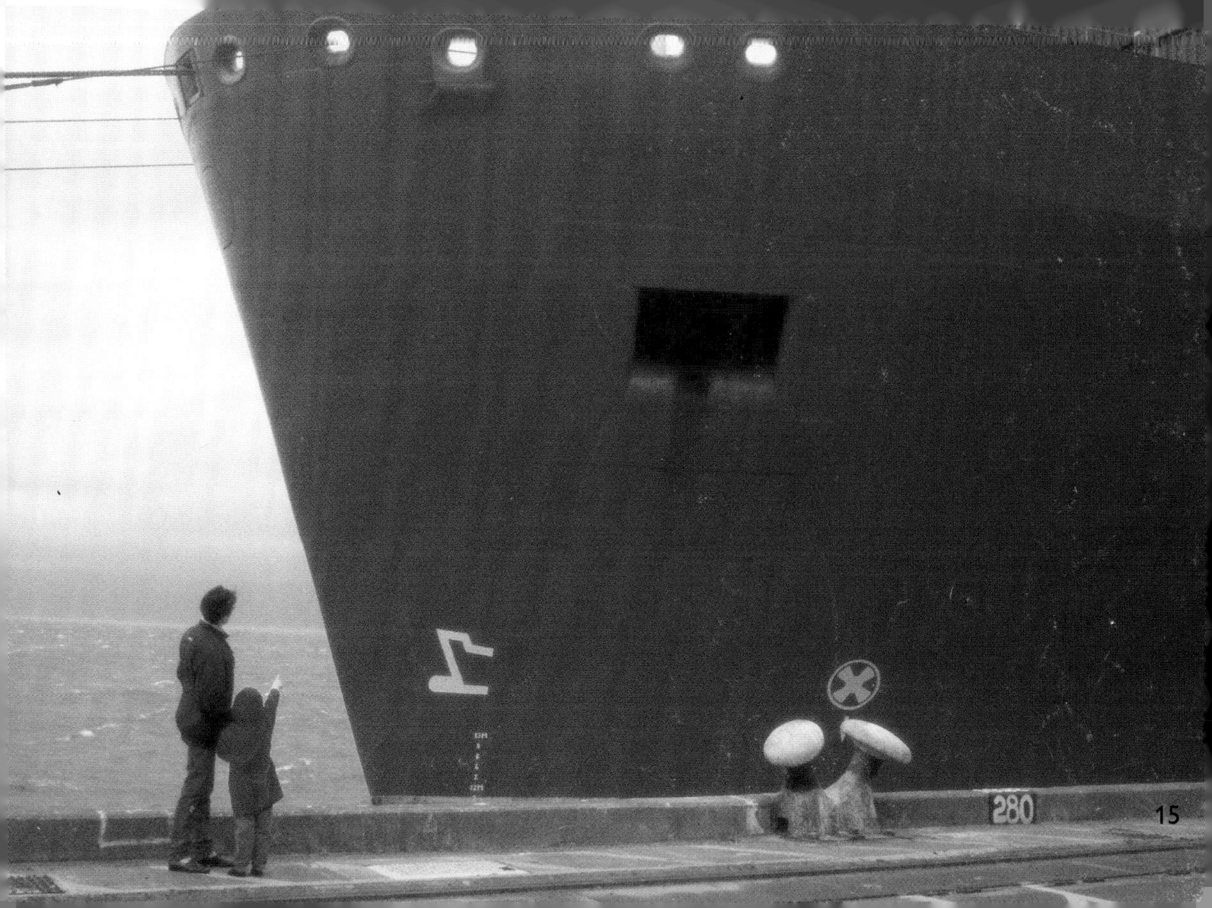
280

A plane is big.

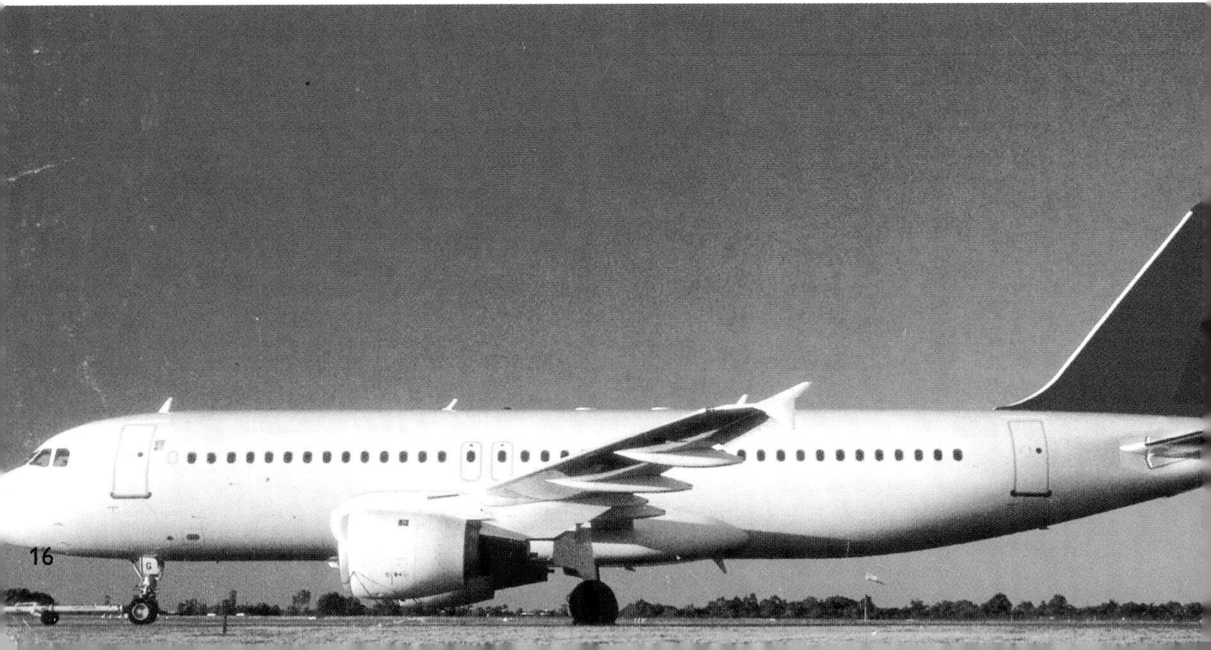